TWO CELLOS

BEAUTIFUL MUSIC FOR TWO STRING INSTRUMENTS

by Samuel Applebaum

VOLUME IV

FOREWORD

The study of string instruments should include ensemble playing at the earliest possible stage. There is much to be gained from the playing of duets. Each player learns how to listen to the other, and in a short time develops an awareness of balance, musical phrasing, intonation and tone quality. This type of training is excellent preparation for participation in large groups.

These four volumes of duets for two cellos will help fill the need for early ensemble experience in the public schools. They should be used in string classes as a supplement to any of the standard string methods. They will also encourage music-making outside of the school, with parents or with other students. These duets are ideal for recitals in the public schools and in public school Festivals. They may be played by two performers, or by multiple performers on each part, with or without piano accompaniment.

These duets may be played by any combination of string instruments, such as:

Two Violins	**Violin and Viola**	**Viola and Cello**	**Cello and Bass**
Two Violas	**Violin and Cello**	**Viola and Bass**	
Two Cellos	**Violin and Bass**		
Two Basses			

EXPLANATION OF THE SIGNS USED IN THIS BOOK

⊓ means down-bow. V means up-bow.

A note with a dot above means that the martelé bowing is to be used. These notes are to start with a sharp accent and end with a clean stop. Each note should be clearly enunciated.

Notes marked with dots might also mean that the spicato bowing is to be used. When the spiccato bowing is required it will be indicated by the abbreviation "spicc."

When there are two notes in one bow that are marked with dashes. we leave a slight pause between each note. They are not to be played as sharply as if marked with dots. Stress each note slightly but with the tone remaining continuous. This is called portato.

A note marked with a dot and a dash is to be played smoothly but slightly shortened in length, followed by a slight pause. In other words, the note is to be held a bit less than its full value.

A cross (+) above a note means left-hand pizzicato. The number above the (+) will tell you which finger to use to pluck the open string.

A fermata (𝄐)or hold above a note means that the note should be held a little longer than its value.

A.M. means to play above the middle of the bow. B.M. means to play below the middle of the bow.

W.B. means whole bow. (This term is approximate).

The two slanted lines (//)mean that the bow is to be lifted from the string. While it is frequently used at the completion of a phrase when it ends up-bow the bow may also be lifted for technical convenience such as before skipping strings or to prepare for the spiccato stroke, etc. It is also helpful in developing a violinistic style.

The comma (9) means a slight pause, also usually at the end of a phrase, with the bow remaining on the string. This usually occurs when the phrase ends on the down-bow above the middle of the bow.

p means soft. ***mp*** means moderately soft. ***pp*** means very soft.

f means loud. ***mf*** means moderately loud. ***ff*** means very loud.

Cresc. or < means gradually louder. Dim. or > means gradually softer. Rit. means gradually slower.

The small square notes indicate that the finger is to be placed on two strings. This square note is to be stopped by the fingers but not played. It makes it possible to go from one string to another smoothly. Observe this only when it is possible for the player to do so.

The measures are numbered according to phrases and should be studied by the players. As a general rule, the melody should be played a bit stronger than the accompanying part, except when the two voices move together in 3rds, 6ths or octaves.

The duets are carefully chosen and arranged to provide technical benefit and musical enjoyment. Each duet may be played twice with the partners changing parts.

E.L.2228

Use the spiccato bowing on the eighth notes marked with dots. When a note is marked with a dot and a dash it is to be played smoothly but held less than its full value. Notes that are not marked or those with dashes are to be played with a smooth détaché stroke.

1. A Lively Dance

Moderately fast-with spirit (Key of C)

W. A. MOZART

E.L.2228

Aim for beautiful tone quality as well as accuracy in intonation. When playing double-stops, incline the bow slightly towards the lower string.

2. Meditation

C. DANCLA

Slowly-with religious feeling (Key of G)

The quarter notes marked with dots are to be played with the martélé stroke. From measure seventeen on, the melody should be played below the middle of the bow in order to use the spiccato stroke on the last three eighth notes in the measure.

3. A Stately Minuet

F. J. HAYDN

[Melody]
33
37
41
45
49
53
57
61
B.M.
2nd
3rd
1st
4th
5th
mf
rit.
[Melody]

Play the sixteenth notes with a broad, smooth détaché stroke with each note clearly enunciated. The eighth notes marked with dots and dashes are to be played warmly, with vibrato, leaving a slight pause between each note.

4. A Two Part Invention

J. S. BACH

5. A German Dance

W. A. MOZART

Moderate fast-gaily (Key of G)

p B.M. 1st *f spicc.* [Melody]

[Melody] *p* B.M. 1st *spicc.*

f [Melody]

The spiccato stroke is to be used on the eighth notes marked with dots, particularly when they serve as an accompaniment to the melody. Use the wrist when going from one string to another for the legato accompaniment, as for example, from measure seventeen on.

6. Concertante

F. MAZAS

Moderately fast-majestically (Key of D)

[Melody]
half
spicc.
B.M.
a tempo
rit.
cresc.
W.B.
Tip
A.M.

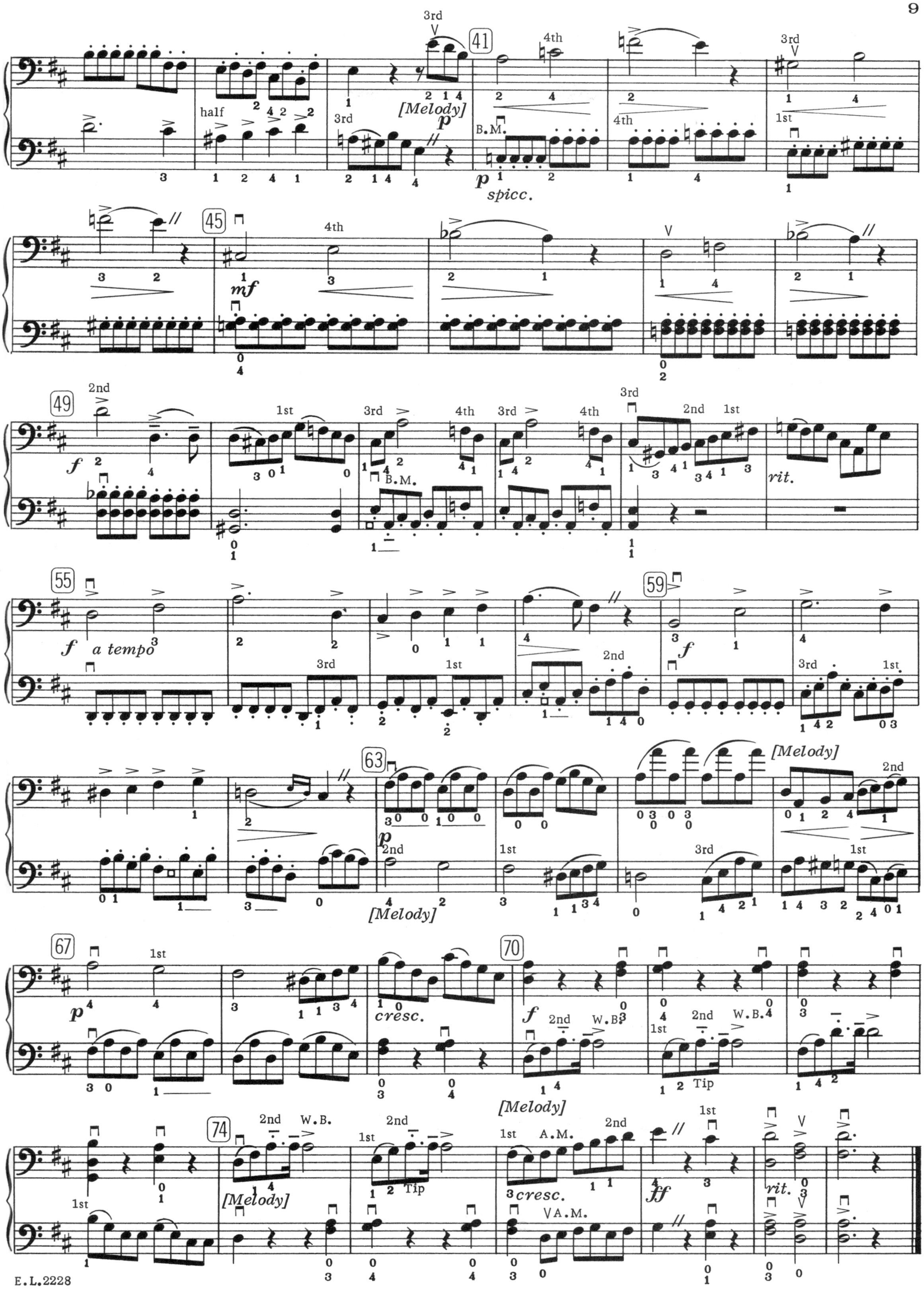

1. A Sarabande is a stately dance probably of Spanish origin, in slow 3/4 or 3/2 time. The second note is usually prolonged throughout the second and third beats of the measure.
2. This number is to be played with vigor and breadth of style. Notice the E flat in the second chord of the third measure.

7. Sarabande

37
spicc.
1st
cresc.
2nd
41
A.M.
W.B.
ff
45
4th
ff
rit.
2nd
ff
rit.
tr
a tempo
Fine
52
p Tenderly and calmy
a tempo
half
3rd
56
pp
p
60
p
[Melody]
64
pp
mf
rit.
D. C. al Fine
ff
D. C. al Fine

In measure three, as well as in similar measures, stay below the middle of the bow so as to be ready for the series of up-bow spiccatos. Lift the bow between each note. The sixteenth notes are to be played broadly and smoothly, using less bow when they are marked piano (*p*).

8. Fantasy

30
dolce
[Melody]
34
cresc.
36
39
B.M.
spicc.
44
48
52
tr.
54
56
58
rit.

1. A Canzonetta is a light, lyrical piece, much in the character of a dance song, usually in two or three parts.
2. Use the spiccato stroke on all the notes marked with dots whether they are eighths or sixteenths.

9. Canzonetta

C. DANCLA

43
cresc.
[Melody]
48
2nd
1st
f
dim.
3rd
p
mf
52
f
p
f
56
p
f
dim.
61
rit.
p a tempo
[Melody]
65
cresc.
2nd
f
dim.
p
D. C. al Fine
[without repeats]

In this duet the spiccato stroke is to be used on the sixteenth notes marked with dots and the martelé for the eighth notes marked with dots. The mordents are to be played as a single trill, using the note above and then back to the original note.

10. Sonatina

C. P. E. BACH

28
3rd
5th
1st
B.M.
spicc.
32
2nd
half
36
4th
40
44
47
51
55

Carl Stamitz, like his father was a famous violinist and composer, born May 7, 1746. He wrote operas, symphonies and much chamber music. His brother Anton was the teacher of the Rudolphe Kreutzer who wrote the famous etudes for the violin.

11. Duet - In The Style Of Mozart

CARL STAMITZ

38
43
48
51
55
59
62
65
68
1st
half
2nd
4th
rit.
a tempo
[Melody]

An example of the staccato bowing will be found in measure five. When this bowing occurs, it is to be played above the middle of the bow using the full width of the hair. Each player should listen carefully to the other so that the notes sound together and the same amount of bow is used.

12. Caprice

LEOPOLD MOZART

If you play this duet with a violin, a cut is to be made on the violin part from the last beat of measure 27 to the last beat of measure 42. Use the spiccato bowing on all 8th notes marked with dots. The violin part is so written that the music is placed on a table and performed with the players facing each other.

13. Table Music For Two

Moderately fast-with spirit (Key of G)

W. A. MOZART

In this canon, the second player begins when the first reaches the second measure, which is marked with a sign. The second player ends on the first note in measure forty-six, which is marked with a fermata. The first player ignores the fermata and goes on to the end.

14. A Canon In Unison

G. TELEMANN

In this duet, the second cellist plays the same notes as the first, a measure later and frequently an octave lower.

15. A Canon In Octaves

This duet is to be played with repose, vibrating on the quarter notes as well as on the longer notes. Increase the speed of the vibrato for passages of greater intensity, as from fifty-five to fifty-nine.

16. Nocturne

Slowly-in a sustained manner (Key of G)

CHAS. de BERIOT

[Melody]

cresc.

[Melody]

cresc.

[Melody]

dim.

[Melody]

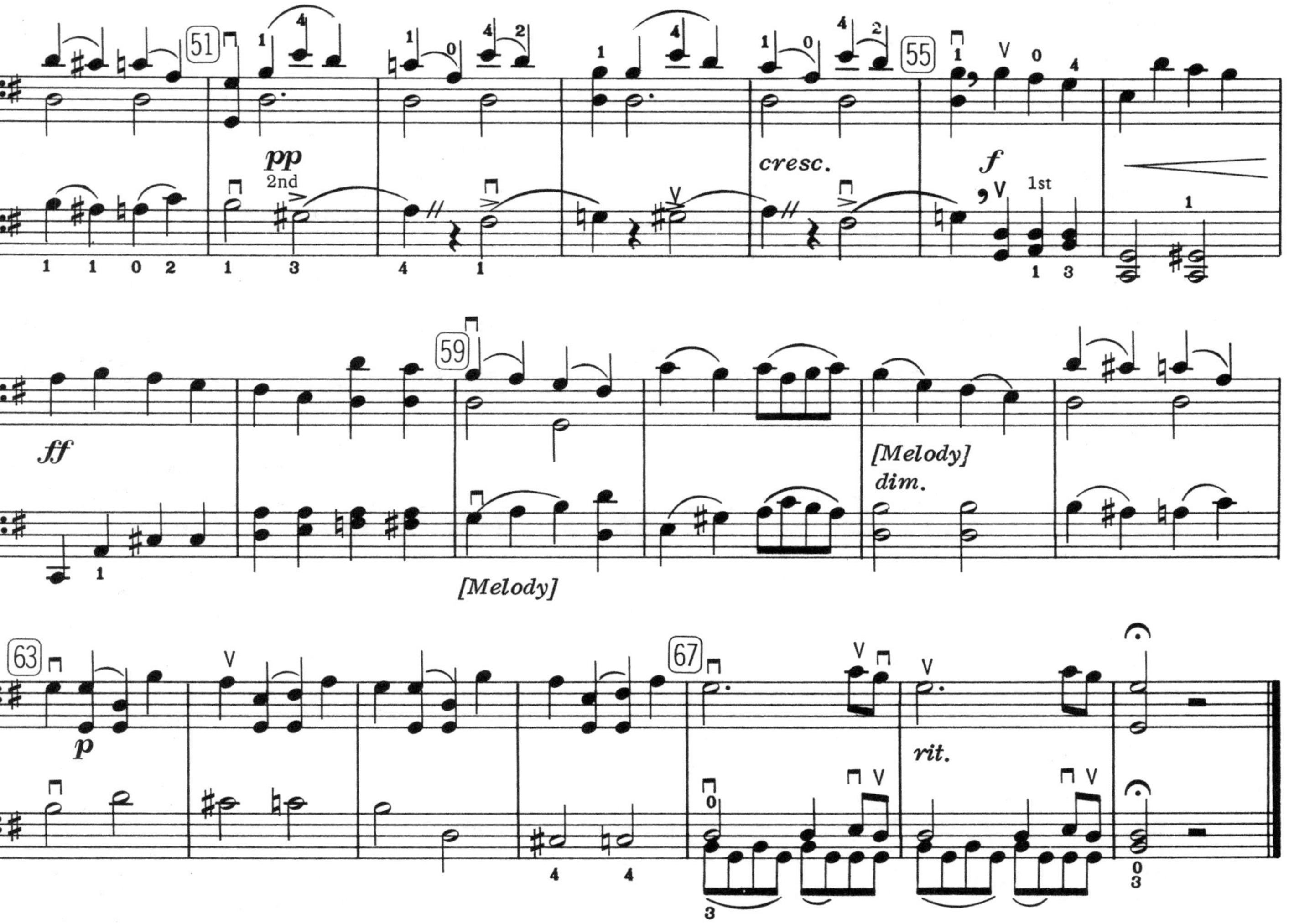

pp cresc. f ff [Melody] [Melody] dim. p rit.

17. A Bit Of Old Vienna

In moderate time-in the style of a minuet (Key of C)

B. TOURS

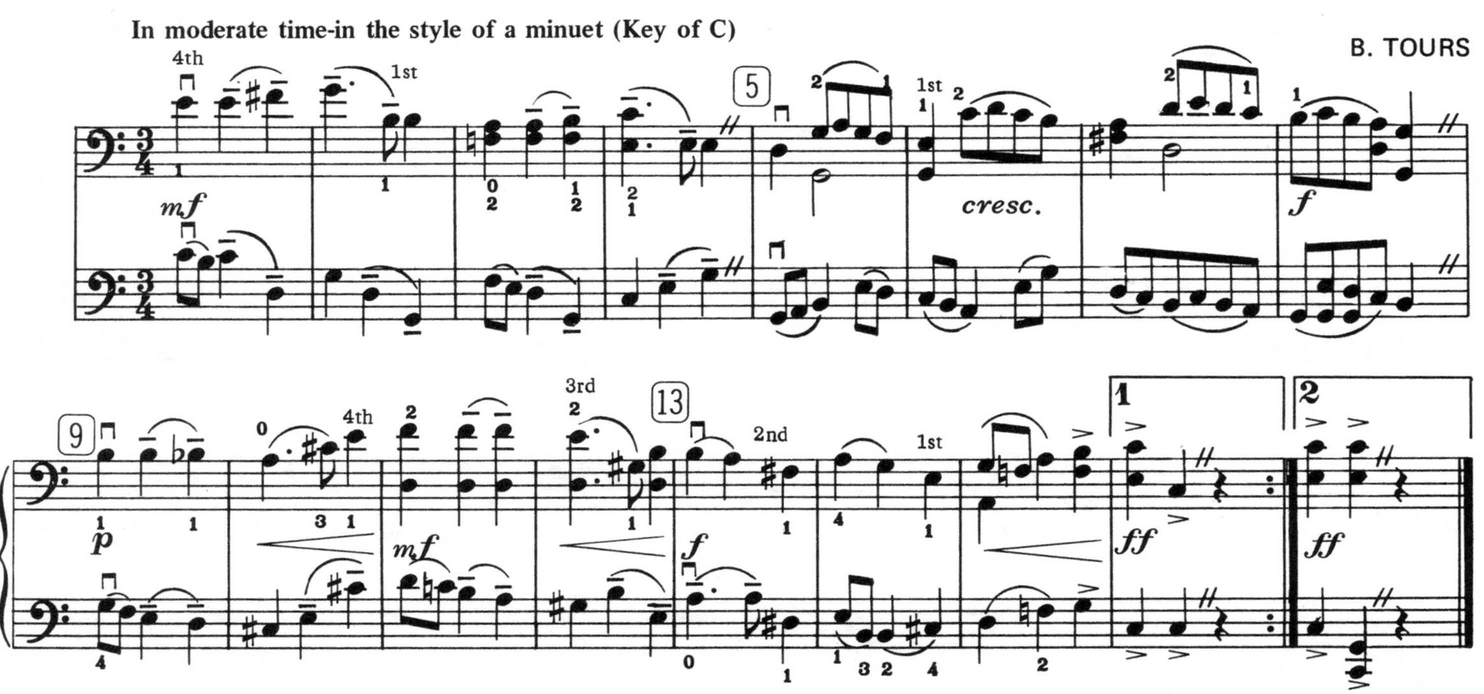

A Rondo is a dance form in which the original theme is repeated several times. Between each repetition, this main theme alternates with several episodes or contrasting passages. In this Rondo, the main theme is played in the first sixteen measures, then again from measures fifty-three through sixty-eight, and then from measures eighty-five through one hundred.

18. Rondo

F. C. NEUBAUER

Moderately fast-brightly (Key of C)

53
57
2nd
1st
61
65
mf
69
2nd
[Melody]
1st
73
4th
3rd
77
85
89
93
f [Melody]
97
101
Coda
rit.

Where there are two small slurs in a large slur, play all the notes in the same bow. Allow for a slight break in the tone, however, between the two small slurs, with each player using the same length of bow, as for example in measure twenty-three.

19. Duo No. 2

P. NARDINI

[Melody]
half
[Melody]
rit.

This duet is fugal in character. The theme is announced again a fourth above starting from the third beat of the fourth measure. When the main theme occurs, it should be brought out a bit stronger than the other voice. Notice that in measures four and twelve, it starts on the third beat of the measure. In measures twenty-three and thirty-one it starts on the first beat of the measure.

20. Gaiety

G. TELEMANN

half
2nd
dim.
1st
28
p
cresc.
31
f
37
3rd
41
4th
46
49
ff
rit.
tr.